poetry **south**

Poetry South 1

ISBN 978-1-906309-04-6

First published September 2007 by Pighog Press & THE SOUTH

THE SOUTH.
Brighton Writers' Centre
49 Grand Parade
Brighton BN2 9QA
UK
www.thesouth.org.uk
info@theesouth.org.uk

pighog
PO Box 145
Brighton BN1 6YU
UK
www.pighog.co.uk

Design by Curious
www.curiousdesign.com

Poetry South 1
Autumn 2007

Foreword

Ron Silliman wrote of his own work that he did not seek a synthesis but a melee. This collection offers just that – a melee and one that provides us with a unique starting point in celebrating the diversity of contemporary poetry being written in the south. It presents new work from fifteen of the south's liveliest writers. Some names here are familiar, many long established, indeed revered, Jackie Wills, John Agard, Brendan Cleary and Catherine Smith but others are new to us reflecting the evolving face of a vibrant, if disparate, southern poetry scene. Over many years the familiar names have had a significant impact on the direction of new writing and this volume is testament to their long standing support and enthusiasm.

Within we find the sonnet, villanelles, free verse, prose poetry, a double haiban, the comic, the political, autobiographical, elegaic and the surreal. Subjects include a Breton wedding dress, an empty train, the most beautiful man on Spetse and cricket, whilst our surroundings find us in a hospital, in a shed, in Sussex, Toledo, Poland, Greece, Zimbabwe and Old Kasa.

With this collection comes a set of contributors' notes that provide a unique insight into the way the poets think about their work, what stimuli trigger that initial urge to write, how a poem evolves, and what force moves the idea forward. The comments are rich, often passionate and provide a wonderful backdrop against which to enjoy the poems.

Contents

John Agard

A wider sense of loss can often crystallise itself in a poem around a solitary moment, memory, even object. In the case of the traumatic floods that hit Lewes and other areas, home and livelihood were both affected. For example, legendary greengrocer Bill, was one of those flood-hit both in terms of home and business, but he managed to bounce back with admirable energy and commitment. One friend of ours, Serena, told how the water level reached the top of her grand piano – which for me was a graphic picture of water's insidious fury. Memory of the flood and the sense of loss came to crystallise itself around that image. And thinking of the piano, almost as a kind of endangered creature, led me down the road the poem took. Along the way, my mind flashed to D.H Lawrence's recollection of his mother in his Piano poem ('Softly, in the dusk, a woman is singing to me').

The poem about the piano lost to the flood was written years ago but it's good to live with poems for a while. As regards the other piano poem ('A Man From The Far Right Is Having A Nightmare'), I didn't consciously set out to write another piano poem, but years later, a line came to my head – the racist is having a nightmare. And my teenage daughter was amused by the idea of a piano being in hot pursuit of such a person. Again, I lived with the poem a while, never quite happy with the word 'racist' which I felt, in the context of the poem, was too simplistic, maybe too neat, too clear-cut, when people are far more complex. Then the thought came, how about the piano chasing a man from the Far Right?

John Agard was born in Guyana and came to Britain in 1977. He has published a number of collections of poetry for children and adults. He was the first writer-in-residence at the South Bank Centre in 1993 and at the BBC in 1998. His most recent adult collection, WE BRITS (Bloodaxe Books) received a Decibel shortlist as part of the Galaxy Awards 2007. Maura Dooley has said of his work; 'His poems are direct and arresting, playful, full of startling imagery, and hilarious, passionate and erotic as often as they are political – often managing to be all these things at once.'

For A Piano Lost In The Lewes Flood: October 2000

For Serena

Not an amphibian
but a creature of land.

Natural habitat:
drawing room
school hall
concert stage
pub corner
where it waits
to be stroked.

Responds to
a child's one-fingered
virtuoso chopsticks.
A maestro's
measured frenzy.
A mother's singing
in the dusk.
Someone's sudden
appassionato
into the past.

Not a creature
equipped for
rising water
and a river's
ever widening hands.
Not a creature
meant to squat
in a river's crescendo.

No, a creature
rooted to land
on upright legs,
though in a movie
they once moved one
down the Amazon.
But this is real life

in a Sussex town,
and this is the river Ouse
drawing on
its ancient source,
and this is my friend
Serena's grand piano
- a victim
at the altar
of the element
that consumes
as it cleanses.

A Man From The Far Right Is Having A Nightmare

His sleep is in a state of vertigo.
He's being pursued by a piano.
One of those grand concert hall affairs
intended for a maestro
is after him
          up the stairs
          down the stairs
          but where are the stairs
          and why do they lead nowhere?
His legs can't compete with legs of rosewood
Or for that matter mahogany
And what's that tinkling in his blood?
Looks like there's no escaping
          those integrated ivories
          that snap at his heels
          and seem to mock
          his mobility.
Those rows of black and white teeth
grinning all their sharps and flats
mistaking his tossing and turning for middle C.
If only he could regain submission
to a peaceful pentatonic sleep.
Enough of this harmonic progression
screams the man from the Far Right.
Thank God for alarm clocks and daylight
that restore black to black and white to white.

Dust

Sweep me under the carpet. Still I fly.
I'm a cosmos in a microscope's eye.
I form galaxies out of surfaces.
Surrender gracefully to my traces.
No respecter of any boundary,
my minuscule footsteps make no fanfare,
yet I'll enter the pores of a city
as easily as your skin or hair.
Dare to dismiss me as mere particle.
I bridge visible and invisible.
Kick me up, and you create confusion.
Bite me, and you embrace oblivion.
To return to me is your lifelong trek.
I whose sovereignty begins with a speck.

Pigeon Politics

See how they brood
on brooding bronze
See how they perch
on posterity's chosen

See how their dripping medals
decorate all pedestals.

Tim Beech

Tim Beech was born in Cannock, Staffordshire in 1953. He was educated at Cannock Grammar School, Flintshire College of Technology and the University of Salford where he gained a Ph.D. in physical chemistry. He currently works as shepherd/ estate worker on Lullington Heath National Nature Reserve. He has a pamphlet of poetry, 'A Solitary Pine Tree in Sussex', published by Pighog Press and is a member of Footwork, the collective of Sussex poets.

He writes: "As with much that I have written 'Nightjar at Springslade Lodge' is an attempt to form a synthesis between the concrete and the abstract; not necessarily thematically nor as metaphor – it may simply be an observation or experience juxtaposed with whatever thoughts preoccupied me at the time. In the case of this poem there is a clear link between St. Augustine's belief that the souls of the unbaptized were irredeemably condemned to eternal damnation with the old legend described in the piece."

Nightjar At Springslade Lodge

Out of the almost perfect solitude of night
A faint churring rises then falls, shifting
Around the edge of the dark plantation

Augustine's 'logical consistency
Parvulos in damnatione omnium
Unearthly bird; the souls of the unbaptized

Carried forever in the still, dark air
Borne lightly on your silent lilting wings.

Night Train

Tired eyes reflect back from the windows,
A low murmur in some unknown tongue
As we cross the river by Blackfriar's bridge,
The monks looking on in silence.

The dark water cuts insistent lights,
Its depth reflective of some broken force.
Endurance. The salmon, they say, have returned
To battle upstream, to spawn and to die.

By paradox, static and ponderous,
The river moves me and leaves me the same;
Its great depth reflecting an absence
That flows into a presence somewhere else.

My eyes are blank, withdrawn into themselves:
Memories flicker for a while then fade away.

At Long Bridge

The nightingale no longer sings
                                        by the reed bed
Where the river is an absence.
And my heart fast in the owl's grip
And my blood mingling
                                        with wet earth
Seeps away and is lost.

A grey heron stalks
                                        the far bank
Waiting for the question.
And there is nothing to be said
And shadows of night form
                    in low hollows
Where silence gathers.

The fox finds an easy meal
                                        by the reed bed,
A rib bone in moonlight.
And an otter wanders the far bank
And the owl shrieks
                                        in the hedgerow,
Calling for her mate.

March

1934

In the beginning is the end – Winter
Is not yet finished, the east wind unhindered.
Across the North Sea dark clouds threaten snow

Without war, some say, there can be no peace.
In Pontefract, a collier's son, slight but tough
Gains a scholarship to grammar school.

The axioms of Euclid, a straight line
Extending to infinity, certainties
Within a shifting world; untimely, lost.

1944

Across a vast horizon, desert sands,
A wilderness featured only by mirage,
The tangible dissolved to a hazy glow,

You fly north on a triangle of vectors;
A compass bearing adjusted to wind speed
And direction: the way forward and back.

That here you met death cannot be doubted.
And yet you kept faith, did not betray
The silence of those touched by fire and blood.

2006

The wind has backed south-westerly, warm and wet.
A skylark sings: chaffinches squabble and fight.
The winter's power recedes. Memory fades.

You lived at one remove, remote and lonely,
A suffering you would never let me share,
Forever an exile in your own land.

It is eight years now since death came to you,
Seeping blood into your brain: and yet you live
Entangled in my mind; forever lost.

Brendan Cleary

Originally from Co Antrim, Brendan now lives in Brighton, where he works as a poet and poetry tutor. Over a period of twenty years he has published five full-length poetry collections, 'White Bread and ITV' (Wide Shirt Press, 1990), 'The Irish Card' (Bloodaxe Books,1994), 'Sacrilege' (Bloodaxe Books, 1998) 'Stranger In The House' (Wrecking Ball Press, 2001) and 'Weightless' (Tall Lighthouse, 2005). 'The Poets' Notebook', his handbook of advice on writing and editing poetry that offers guidance on the creaive process for any artist is published by Pighog Press www.pighog.co.uk. He has also published many pamphlets from numerous small presses. He has performed his poetry throughout the UK and Ireland for many years.

The poems included here form part of a forthcoming collection of autobiographical work rooted in family history. Whereas Brendan is known for his use of persona here the speaking voice is his own. All the poems are dedicated to the memory of Martin Cleary, who died November 24th 1975.

The Dead

when Robbie's Da died the whole family
were gathered around her bedside
not like you disappearing off the scale
as the beeps & machines cascaded in
& I remember Joe McClenahan well
spitting gobs of phlegm into the fire
supping his soup too soon between fags
saying 'it would scald the bake off a papist'
& and he probably missed you in the Dolphin
after Abbey Meats gave you your cards
& you had to sign on & were all at sea
so declared your work as the head waiter
so got fuck all moneywise but Joe was sad
& so was Dorothy Davidson & Mrs Hill
who you met through Peg after the war
so if we could arrange a heavenly choir
I'd listen to all of these dead people sing
poor dead provider of the seed in me

With acknowledgements - written in the south, first published in The North.

At The Grave

a fierce wind slashes through
just about everything
& there's a mist over Larne Lough
& Mama is nearly 83 now
so doesn't get about much
& has to bring a stick
but we've managed a trip
to traipse around charity shops
get some oven chips from Dunnes
some peanut cookies in Iceland
& two bundles of carnations
we've brought for you here
& she's trimming them at the skip
while I'm off looking for the tap
so we place them in a rusty vial
before we head home & she reckons
they'll be strewn all over the place
& as the rain starts to fall
over Magheramorne
I notice how worn your name is
& your dates on the stone

The Premonition

Bohemian Rhapsody
was never off the radio
even on that Sunday
I met you & Mama
walking arm-in-arm
down the Chapel Hill
& I knew it then
an instinct I fought
down on the promenade
thinking about stuff
like the old reel to reel
Nurse Curry gave me
or the glass near the bath
with your dentures inside
or maybe five years before
my album of Texaco coins
of my World Cup squad
& the night Uwe scored
with that deft back header
so I went outside fed up
kicking my Wembley ball
against the front gate
sometimes glancing inside
where you sat at the match
thinner & somehow intact
before they made you reduntant
up at the meat plant in Whiteabbey
or before any of the sickness
started to grow around your heart

Christmas 1975

at Alan Morrison's party
with hardly any girls
in his parents bungalow
up the Raw Brae
someone played John & Yoko
'Happy Xmas war is over"
so I put down my can
of Newcastle Brown
& slunk off alone
to Alan's bedroom
crying bucketfuls
staring at the floor
where his new album
by Richard Thompson
'Henry the Human Fly'
stared back at me
& Sean came in
to see I was alright
& I told him I wasn't
because I couldn't forget
you standing in a doorway
at Lourdes school social
singing 'The Old Bog Road"
& 'The mountains of Mourne
sweep down to the sea'
so then I started to drink
to keep your voice
your eyes & bald head
your Ulster Fry belly
your laugh & kind spirit
as far away as possible
until now after 30 years
you walk behind me
a calm shadow
a friendly ghost
or driving your Ford Anglia
or burning my toast for me
in your old dressing gown

Tom Cunliffe

Tom comes from Ellesmere Port, Cheshire. He is a painter/printmaker, a member of Footwork and lives in Hove.

A blackbird sings at 2am. One's first thought is where's the gun? But the song is mysterious and wonderful. The same bird woke me for nights on end and this reminded me of a more ominous occasion when I was awoken, years ago, in the landscape near Siena.

'You might think' started in the usual manner, masses of loops and asterisks but its roots emerged months earlier in my email spam. Some of the short titles fascinated me (it was if someone had randomly taken a pin to a dictionary) so I began collating them, eventually drawing them together and using them with improvised music. I find the way words, phrases, and images are misconstrued intriguing and some of my recent work has developed into what I call poems of misunderstanding which says of a poem 'it's somewhere in this area' rather than saying 'this is definitely the intention of the poem'.

I like accident, and error, and do not shift to keyboard until late in the creative process. In 'You might think' I typed up the first draft leaving in many repetitions, deferring judgement till later, but as I focussed on reading the work aloud the repetitions, and the staccatto pulse – similiar to that found in my spam – seemed appropriate to the building mood, so I let the idea run.

Arrival

An island has settled outside my home,
it's been on a long journey
          collecting souls.
I'm tempted to open the shutters,
invite it in but
how do you keep the songbirds out?

I'd like to keep it
but the only things I've ever stolen are books.
Perhaps I could conceal it between pages
          or camouflage it,
as if one were painting
the dark side of the moon
                              white.

Poem *(Zimbabwe)*

3rd person personal pronoun

possessive pronoun.....noun....verb...interrogative pronoun...noun
indefinite article...noun...preposition.....noun...indefinite article.....noun
verb...possessive adjective... noun...verb ...noun
verb...adverb...conjunctive...possessive pronoun...noun...fullstop.

stanza break

noun ...verb...indefinite article...conjunctive...noun
noun..?????.......adjective...conjunctive...noun...hyphen....noun...adjective
?????....noun ...verb...conjunctive... definite article...noun
verb...conjunctive...definite article...noun...exclamation mark...end

...........(censored)

Confluence

The clocks without fingers are decoys, striking as they do at irregular times. Workers leave continually, rushing quietly over the bridge, beneath which joggers sleep or run, and old men cuddle. Children, with their birds are tucked up in bed. Listening, glass to the wall, one becomes more suspicious of good manners.
Where she wades in naked you can just make out the blind fish.

into the night
old men practice t'ai chi
others swim in circles

A cassoulet of shoes covered the floor, little voices of anxiety nibbling their toes. The last of the hail swept the tall windows flushing the empty square, tailing leaves away like disappointed football fans escaping a match early. Straight-faced adjudicators shuffled about the room discussing imaginary paintings, peering down to record the artist's name asking, Where does the soul abide?
He recalled beating sheets on the balcony, reading out his mandate to those assembled below; one pair of bejewelled stiletto boots to each inhabitant, one sable gown per rider, the game of chess to be ignored. She was watching the adjudicators sharing a joke behind their palms. It was at that point she started counting.

they lie open mouthed
on a bed of dust
little journeys

you might think

you might think   night bird like yap
piercing the canvas   a shock suddeness and   into dog silence
coming across the fields   from the veranda ... patio
it happened a long time ago   she sleeps on   the scrutiny of waiting
I doze   sounds violate   moving across

again from the foliage   silence is inaction   screams carry
a frieze of trees   a dog fox calling his troop   a hollow piping
around her throat   a breaking yelp   stretched out   beneath the canvas
cloth wiped air   the order of olive trees

tender border of cow parsley and bramble   her legs open in dry leaves
yellow squall   through fields and pools   chatter disrupted
the accoustic orchard   silent hives   following cries   sounds violate

days sleep   it happened a long time ago   a vixen coming around
barks mutate   chorus   stroking her throat   the fox bickers
shaped and bolting loose   severance of voice   infant stoniness

John Davies

John Davies published his first pamphlet collection 'The Nutter in the Shrubbery' in 2002. In the same year he won an ArchiTEXTS Award for his first residency as Shedman (www.shedman.net) and he set up THE SOUTH to produce seven special ACE funded commissions for poets working with visual artists on the theme 'place of birth'. He has received an Arts Council England personal development award and his poetry has been published in anthologies and magazines and he has read his work at events and festivals in the UK, Ireland and Europe. His full length collection 'Shedman' is published by Pighog www.pighog.co.uk.

"A commissioned piece, 'Earthed' was inspired by a photograph of Firle Shoulder in winter but is based on my need for the comfort of the ground when my mother died. I was fascinated by the poetic power of the names found in the landscape itself which read like a spell. 'Perspective', another commission, went through nine main drafts and came out of a long conversation with Victor Stuart Graham, a textile artist who now works mainly with driftwood. His artistry and biography, the curious light shed on the quay at Newhaven and my own exploration of the so-called numinous came together in a poem written over a week, then revisited many times later for tiny adjustments. The last line came to me with treacherous certainty.

'Dragon' came from the idea that everyone has an unfinished project in their shed and deliberately plays against Brian Patten's well known poem with the same title all about love.

Once I'd heard the first line of 'Clothes of Grey' in my head, the poem evolved over a period of hours as part of a challenging, intense but enjoyable mental exercise, a bit like a jigsaw or crossword puzzle, but with a huge emotional pull too, as I unearthed what the woman at the heart of the poem was trying to say. I edited it and lived with it over the next year, making minor corrections and testing it out at readings. Within the poem's structural container themes I often explore float to the surface – change and response to it, expectation, reversal, anger."

Earthed

The day I sheltered there, there was no snow,
though snowy hair and winter thoughts had drawn
me up past Tilton Wood and Pearson's Wish.
That autumn day I lay down at the foot
of Bostal Hill, a miniature of all that lay above,
and cried away my grief and all my love.

The rhythm of the chalk, its roll and turn,
held me in a strong and timeless trance,
the comfort of the ground beneath Bo Peep
and Jerry's Pond. She who once was frozen
stone naps now in the hill, the giantess
asleep before she wakes to dance.

Tilton Wood, Pearson's Wish, Bostal Hill, Bo Peep and Jerry's Pond are all place names on or near Firle Shoulder on the South Downs near Firle, East Sussex.

Perspective

For Victor Stuart Graham

His favourite structure is the light shed on its rusty rails,
the relic of an ancient railway that ran over, not along, the river.
Its light marks the spot where train, driver, passengers, de-materialised.
It's a knack we've somehow lost, which is why we mark the spot.

His talent with driftwood, fasteners, string, stems from years
of painting railings with his dad, as if the even temper, i.e. boredom
of the work, launched his trajectory of imaginings. I see him now
a stripling of sixteen, dabbing a brush into a pot with a thin wire handle.

Did a passing quinquireme train his eye or something dirty, British,
plodding down the channel? Through all those days of dreamy brushings,
all those mindless afternoons, did the sea etch its patterns on his mind
so that now every grain is cloud or wave, every shape a disguised ship?

They find release in his hands, resurrected to a new dimension
where wood's every ambition is fulfilled. To be a supertanker or a tug.
To be a seagull or a Christmas tree. To be a light shed on its rusty rails
and indicate a miracle. The possibilities immense, when you're wood.

Dragon

With acknowledgements to Brian Patten's A Small Dragon

It's sitting in the corner of your shed,
sad eyed and legless. "You love me," it says.
Many's the day you've ignored its mournful look
crossing the threshold from what once was
to what might have been. "I love you," it says,
and tries to get up on its little stumps, but falls.
Sometimes you pick it up; more often watch
it crawl back to its patient corner where it moons
for days. "Love you more," it simpers. In its eyes
flash a hundred dreams and promise just about
to be fulfilled. The day you turf it out, it glowers
at you, silently, in the hatchback to the dump.

Clothes of Grey

The dusk gathers the riders. Do not compare yourself with these.
Why, they feel nothing. Do not dwell or hanker. Do not follow their
clothes of grey, your vanishing mist, slipping through the trees.

Why do they call you when my love gives you opal, cockatiels, keys
to open and enlighten secret rooms? Why sing in the shadow where
the dusk gathers the riders? Do not compare yourself with these

poor things, they are not real. Where will they lead you? Please
look at me. Where am I in your plans? Tell me. How am I to share
clothes of grey? Your vanishing mist slipping through the trees -

Is that all I will have and hold of us? How can you? How she's
lost him, they'll say, as if I've been careless, when it's just not fair.
The dusk gathers the riders - do not compare yourself with these.

When will you come back? When will your heart unfreeze?
If not for my sake then think of the children. Must they wear
clothes of grey, your vanishing mist? Slipping through the trees

without a word, you coward - you think escaping frees?
We'll see. I'll wear grey silks, the finest underwear. I don't care
the dusk gathers the riders. Do not compare yourself with these
clothes of grey. Your vanishing? Mist slipping through the trees.

Robert Dickinson

I've had poems in various magazines; Szyzgy, a joint collection with Andrew Dilger, was published in 2001. Other works include a comedy, 'Murder's Last Case', which played for a week in 2004, and the libretto for 'Joby Talbot's Path of Miracles', which premiered in 2005.

Most of my poems start from a single idea or collision of two ideas – or the realisation that the line that occurred to me while I was walking back from the shops might serve some purpose after all. The poem itself is not usually written until some time after this realisation, by which time I'll have forgotten the original prompt. This poem is slightly different in that it had a very specific starting point: a footnote in an old Loeb edition of Catullus: Locus desperatus. The emendations proposed are no more than ingenious guesses. This gave me the title and the image of a corrupted text as a metaphor for a different kind of loss. Once I had this, the piece seemed to write itself, though not, as usual, until several years later. The sharp German doctor is Dr. Alois Alzheimer; anachronistic for the Regency, it's true, but anachronism is possibly appropriate for a poem about the failure of memory.

Locus Desperatus

Memory, like a resentful copyist,
drowsing half the day at the scriptorium;
writing *hammer* for *screwdriver,*
yesterday for *today,* pausing at the lost words.

Or a tableau of Regency daughters:
Aphasia, Agnosia, and pallid Alexia,
their suitor the sharp German doctor
whose name is at the tip of all tongues . . .

Memory shakes itself awake, and guesses,
writing down whatever fills the space.

Security

The train runs empty to the empty town.
Its doors slide open to a platform
where gulls ignore the harsh recorded voice.
There is birdshit, newspapers blown in from elsewhere;
sometimes a paper gusts into a carriage,
and, pinned against a seat, the pages turn
to week-old photographs of motorways
blank as dreams or adverts for new cars.
The doors slide shut, the train will ease away,
gathering speed through the suburbs
and level crossings where no-one waits,
to stop again at the hush of the airport
where, beyond barriers and stalled escalators,
a stray dog will cross the departure lounge,
pause for a moment, ears pricked,
then carry on its frantic, starved routine
caught on official cameras, and unseen.

The Fall Of Troy

Forget what you've heard:
Helen, the ten-year siege, the trick with the horse,
none of that happened.
The truth is, Troy fell in a week,
the king fled south.
His court stayed on to kneel before the Greeks.

Give us Helen, and we'll leave.
But there was no Helen,
and they'd forgotten how to leave.
Out on the beach their ships decayed
while they ransacked our kitchens,
looking for a reason to be there,

blunting their axe heads
on linen chests and cellar doors;
stripping the houses bare
of gold, of brass, of iron, then of stone.
And Helen? She was never here,
and Priam died a hundred years ago . . .

Executions and reprisals, executions.
Our king in the south,
calling upon the astonished gods,
an old man wailing in foreign harbours.
And this went on for days, and then for years;
when there was no-one left to kill they called it peace.

Norfolk Conspiracy

They filmed the first moon landing in my field
and over there, they buried Kennedy,
the real Kennedy, back in '62.
I was a kid then, hiding in ditches
as black cars cruised by hedgerows and canals
or parked six deep across the village green,
looking, it was said, for good locations,
for people who would never be believed.
They found us. There were boxes in storage
labelled "Hoffa", "McCartney", and "Monroe" –
I played beside them in Geoff Miller's barn
the summer Jack Oswald's boy went missing –
he came back rich and drank himself to death.
Happier times. Not much has happened since:
crops come and go, and winter clears the fields,
the houses shrink beneath the heavy skies
and, one by one, the old folk disappear.

Hugh Dunkerley

Hugh has published two pamphlet collections, 'Walking to the Fire Tower' (Redbeck Press) and 'Fast' (Pighog Press). He teaches at The University of Chichester and is the West Sussex Poet Laureate. He lives in Brighton and is married to the novelist Bethan Roberts.

Hugh writes 'Love, desire and sexuality. Poets have been writing about these subjects for as long as there has been poetry. So how to do it in a new way? Some of these poems have their origins in actual experiences, while others are wholly fictional. But what links them together, in my mind, is a concern with the strangeness, the almost alien nature of desire, the way it can sweep people up and radically alter their lives without them even understanding what is happening. In 'Coffee', I wanted to suggest this moment of being swept along, hence the use of short lines to suggest urgency. I have also used fractured moments of speech and ellipsis. 'Mussels' and 'Hare' both try to connect what we think of as human nature to the wider sense of nature which is everywhere, within us and without. With 'Brighton', I have used the sonnet, a form which is nearly synonymous with the love poem. However, I hope I have done so in a new way, trying to explore what it means to be intimate with someone but, at the same time, feel that one hardly knows them'.

Brighton

Even as they're making love, he wonders
who she is, her wind-tanned face wracked
with pleasure, his body moving inside hers,
their sweat mingling in the overheated
hotel room. Earlier, on the pier,
she'd pushed him up against an empty
hot dog stand, said she didn't care
who saw but that she wanted him, quickly,
right then and there. He'd pulled away,
blethering something about not being
able to breathe. Now in the bathroom mirror
he notices the crow's feet deepening
around her eyes, grey flecking her hair,
glimpses his own unfamiliar stare.

Coffee

Back at his place
she comes in for coffee
and within minutes
they're tearing at each other's clothes,
her tongue sliding against his,
and then he's inside her,
soft muscles closing round him
I have to get closer to you
and she's putting her hand over her mouth,
stifling her shouts,
and it's gathering in his thighs,
burning away all thought...

When he rolls over she's already half-dressed.
I'm sorry, she says, *I have to go. I'll ring you tomorrow.*
Listening to her drive away
he pictures the darkened house,
her slipping into that other bed.

Long after she's left, the smell of her
still clings to his fingers, his face,
a musk-delicate scent, almost perfumed.

Mussels

In the sink they open slyly,
the occasional shift as one
nudges against another

the only indication that
anything might be alive
inside all that armour plating.

Dropping clacking handfuls
into the already erupting water
where they rattle and bounce

in a burning dance, she argues
they're senseless, denies that
anything so rooted in the plant world

can possibly know pain.
As the tender flesh
melts in their mouths

he remembers the limpets
he hacked as a child
from slippery rocks,

their silkiness, how each
creature shrunk back
helplessly into its shell.

Later, as she opens to him,
he's surprised at the pearly
softness between her legs

imagines himself pushing
through something sub-marine
and infinitely vulnerable.

Hare

To Bethan

Snakes that cast their coats for new
Chameleons that alter hue,
Hares that yearly sexes change.
Fletcher: *Faithful Shepherdess*

I

You were surprised by its huge ears,
alert and stiff in the long grass

its masculine nose,
the lithe terrier-like body.

We were almost on it
when the hare erupted into flight

something more like a deer
than a rabbit in the way it ran

bounding in fast surefooted leaps
across the astonished field

until it veered suddenly, rose into the air
and was gone in the dusk of the wood

leaving only this impression
warm in the still unravelling grass.

II

Warm in the still unravelling sheets,
I run my fingers down your spine

trace the soft vestigial hair of an animal
that only minutes ago I held

bucking in my arms, a fierceness
I'd never imagined, straining for release

a changeling that slipped between my fingers
and was gone with a cry

now resolving itself back into you.

Sarah Jackson

Sarah lives and writes in Brighton, where she is undertaking doctoral research in creative writing at the University of Sussex. Her poems have been published widely in journals that include 'The Rialto', 'Envoi', 'Other Poetry' and 'Interpreter's House'. She is also an Associate Tutor on the Creative Writing and Personal Development Masters degree at Sussex University, and has facilitated writing workshops in mental health and community outreach settings. She is currently working on her first novel.

Of 'Vanishing Twin' Sarah writes "I write most of my poetry in dream-time – when my alarm clock cracks open the space between night and day, and crusty eyed, I write sitting in bed. This is the time when images flow uncensored, blurring imagination with waking life. Later – sometimes hours, sometime days, sometimes months – I return to the poem fully awake, and the crafting begins.

'Vanishing Twin' was written in this way. I woke remembering a feeling of looking for someone or something. Still half-asleep, I recalled a conversation I'd had with a friend the previous day about the 'Vanishing Twin Syndrome', where a multiple-pregnancy foetus dies in the womb and is reabsorbed by the mother. It is said that the surviving child may have the trace of a memory of their 'vanished' twin, growing up with an aching sence of loneliness. That morning, I imagined I had lost my twin, and this is my poem for her".

Albert

He's not seen this before:
the sky flexing, breathing
sucking in the sea like a tongue

so he walks over the stones
down and then out over the great flat
to where the old black pier crumbles

and he stands still beneath the red sky
while the gulls pick for worms –
there's dozens of them, and just him –

watching their claws make W's in the silt;
until he walks away slowly, frightened
for his feet leave no prints in the sand.

Vanishing Twin

For years, I've hid
in a cracked hotel
tipping the moors:

I sleep days, among piles
and piles of laundry;
nights, I steal dreams

wrap them up
in soft white towels
longing for you

my duck egg girl
my vanishing twin.
Do you remember me?

I still feel the ache
of your lidless space
your imprint on my skin.

Momos And Tea

Afterwards, breaking through the skin of a 30 watt beam,
we walked out and into the middle depths of night

and stumbling across a ditch or creek or a child,
we ducked into the Whispering Willow Cafe at the edge of Old Kaza

where a group of bug eyed men and three Israeli tourists
talked in low voices, a dim light humming, then blinking out.

When the waiter lit the candle, he glowed up good and bright;
his face utterly smooth, his eyes creaking a little as they met mine

and glancing up I saw that I was alone inside a dream box
with padded walls and ceiling like the mattress of our bed.

The waiter was very sorry: there was nothing he could give us
except momos and tea, which we ate and drank quickly,

listening to the small sounds of our sipping, before stripping
back the dusty notes, peeling ourselves apart

and slipping back into the darkness that hung there between us,
stumbling on and on through the night.

A Quarter To

The grass is damp and my tights
still flat out on the peach carpet, so I tell you

Hurry. We're early you say, but you know nothing
about nothing. Still, your tongue glints

as we step out into the night.
Twist the bottle, not the cork, I say. Quick –

and you bellow when it shoots up
into the moon's open mouth.

We swallow but the moon spits it back out
and as the cork lands by my feet

I see you peek at my butter toes,
remember earlier, how you'd smiled at my tights –

thick, woollen – you plucking bobbles
from behind my thighs. To distract you now

I tell you about my pancake baby:
Oh, you know nothing

I tell you, she is near see-through and her eyes
are cats-eyes yes and her face is fish-skin

and her mouth is her lips is her hips.
Yes, round and snug, a pancake baby,

pockets of peaches, pillows of cream,
and when she cries, I tell you, she leaks poppy seeds.

Maria Jastrzebska

Maria was born in Warsaw, Poland and grew up in London. She is author of 'Postcards From Poland' (Working Press) 'Home From Home' (Flarestack) and 'Syrena' (Redbeck Press) and was co-editor of 'Forum Polek' a bilingual anthology of women's writing. Her work appears in numerous anthologies and journals, most recently in 'Images of Women' (Arrowhead), 'Apokalipsa' (Slovenia), 'Brand', 'Chroma', 'The Interpreter's House', 'Kirjailija' (Finland), 'Poetry International Web', 'Smiths Knoll', 'Staple'. She founded SOUTH POLE, 'Outskirts' and co-runs Queer Writing South.

I write in English but my first language informs everything I do. I'm interested in memory: both the loss of it – whether individually or collectively - and what steps we take to preserve it. I've always been concerned with borders and boundaries: between countries, cultures, languages, between social and sexual identities, health and illness. It is no accident that as a poet I have found myself irresistibly drawn to that 'in-between' form the prose poem.

'Childhood Moments of the Emigrée' is about my mother and focuses on a single moment during her childhood when she left Poland for a trip abroad. I'm trying to encapsulate a fragment of narrative in snapshot form, while also moving through time; stepping in and out of the frame which contains the fragment. 'The Black Knight' (Zawisza Czarny) is a hero from Henryk Sienkiewicz's historical novel 'The Teutonic Knights'. Winnetou is the Native American Indian hero of Karl May's novel of that title. Both were written at the turn of the nineteenth century.

Seventy Five Per Cent*

As far as the fresh fish stall
but not all the way to Maroccos
and that's on a good day.
Most of the dishes, but not the soup pan
or teacups. Acts One and Two,
home to bed before Act Three.
Three quarters of the way
to an orgasm and then, what?
Sixty seven point five
minutes of a football match
but absolutely no chance
of penalties. Gaps in a jigsaw sky,
where blue pieces are missing.
Painting the walls, no corners.
Mowing most of the lawn
but not that last strip.

* Doctors advise patients recovering from M.E to do seventy five per cent of what they would normally expect to do and then stop to rest.

Childhood Moments Of The Emigrée

Warnings go unheeded. Besides, in the implacable past, people took fewer precautions and the barrier between them was purely space across a proverbial or other times real abyss. So the polar bear is always able to reach its hoary, glittering paw over a ledge and snatch her leather satchel, which falls - slowly it must seem now - into the moat below. There is no kind Black Knight, no Winnetou riding bareback to save her. Only the out of breath zoo keeper, who has to retrieve the clearly expensive, hand-sewn satchel and calm down a yelping group of girls all pointing at the bear; to do so all the while speaking in language they dismiss as much too hard to understand.

She has no idea she will one day live surrounded by it, returning after years to that same country. The strange language which the zoo keeper once spoke to her on a school trip abroad will remain a barrier: deeper than any moat, deeper than the grey sea she will have crossed; than the colour of a polar bear's eyes, as it gazes longingly across at her, whether from hunger or boredom, from its small stony island.

Almost

I saw Trevor getting on the bus, would have got out of my seat
to say hello, but then what? The bus was crowded.

When I see him I remember Simon and the last garden (does he want
reminding?) they planted out. All that dark purple lavender

and marigolds, small cups filled with orange light like spinning tops.
Laid out with such care. Do you still bother? I don't think I could,

I'd let the weeds run riot. The dying know how to live - they have to.
We were almost friends for a while. Then he sold up, moved away.

The last time we spoke he looked much thinner, his head shaved, he
said he was living it up, doing 'too many' (semi apologetic shrug

and smile) drugs. He was in a hurry, too fast for me. I watch
him now climbing upstairs to sit with the smokers.

My Mum In Heaven

I can tell she's in heaven
as Chopin himself- or at least
Artur Rubinstein- is playing the Blüthner.

There are ocelot cubs she can stroke
as much as she wants asleep
in her lap. Instead of angels,

lieutenants and airmen hover round her
vying to light her Mewa's.
Folding doors open out onto orchards

bursting with Reine Claude plums;
'Whiskey Mac' blooms all year
its scent as strong as the resin of pine.

She's with Babcia in the orangerie
sipping Chablis, munching meringues.
Beneath the moon and *You are the one*

are all the English she knows
and, though technically I haven't been
born, she giggles, calling me over.

Grace
Nichols

Grace Nichols, poet and children's writer was born and educated in Guyana. Since moving to Britain in 1977 she has written widely for both adults and children. Her adult books include 'I Is A Long-Memoried Woman' which won the 1983 Commonwealth Poetry Prize; the 'Fat Black Woman's Poems' and 'Sunris' which won the Guyana Poetry Prize. She served as poet-in-residence at the Tate Gallery 1999 to 2000 and received a Cholmondeley Award in 2001.

Of her latest collection, 'Startling The Flying Fish' poet and critic, Michelene Wandor says in Poetry Review; 'Grace Nichols's new book is like coming into the light. From her first collection in 1983, 'I Is A Long-Memoried Woman', she has been a strong presence in the linguistic interweave between the Caribbean and the UK.'

'Bed At Tate' was written in response to Tracy Emin's 'My Bed' which was on display during my residency at the Tate Gallery, London (1999-2000). It was among the exhibits short-listed for the Turner Prize in the gallery upstairs and was arousing a lot of controversy both in the media and in the gallery. Many people were flocking specifically to see that, and the debate was hot, as to whether it was art or not. That Emin had the temerity and vision to show her unmade bed as a work of art (accessorised with unwashed underwear, used condom, etc, etc to make her own statement) made me smile. I thought it was honest. I thought it was bold. A brilliant idea putting 'Bed' centre-stage, a piece of furniture most of us take for granted, despite the fact that the key experiences of life – Sleeping, dreaming, dying, having sex and giving birth, happen in bed.

You can say the poem is a kind of ode to Bed, usually seen as a mundane object, so I wanted to address it in a playfully grand way. At the same time the poem hints at the unsettling reality of our own mortality which I think Tracy Emin was also suggesting by her arrangement of the bed and its objects.

Bed At Tate

Inspired by Tracy Emin's Bed, short-listed for the Turner Prize
Tate Gallery, London 1999

Here you are my prop-of-Morpheus.
The way I like you best – plump-pillowed,
white-draped, causally unmade.

Yet wanting to protect you
like the body of my mother
like Noah's nakedness was filially covered

How you bask and blush
under the scrutiny of this public gaze
your intimate secrets laid bare –

That careless snail of condom
The blood-stained knickers
Your pillow's pubic-slit
In its bird-nest of feathers.
The comforting paraphernalia
Of your scissors, painkillers –
All your attributes to
Sex and birth and death

O never mind the clutch of giggling schoolgirls
My dishevelled divan – at last centre-stage.

Scan

For Kalera

From the genesis of the first beginning
I could write no poems about you.
Words hung around like a choir
of inadequate angels in my head –

Tongued tied before – the weaving blood;
the dreaming fist; tiptoeing around
the chambering-heart;
the miniature breath.

Yet for all this –
My body was a ship
on an ocean full of sharks
becoming dolphins.

Sometimes the white-gilled surgeons
summoned you up from the deep.
I could never decipher, little fish,
the messages you spawned onto a screen.

Only sailing after
On my own calm sheets
Could I pick up, quite clearly,
Your reassuring morse-code beats.

Village-Belle

Once a week the doctor would come
to our village.
(a white flag outside the house secured a visit)
Small sicknesses and crotchety illnesses.

He'd make his rounds –
from flagging house to flagging house.
But in the waiting-room of his eye
was Cousin Vy, gently pulling all the while.

She'd close her small
half-empty cakeshop
awaiting him inside
like a spider awaits a fly –

A forty-somethingish femme fatale
A dubious village-belle
She'd plump the cushions
as herself –

A puff of powder to the crotch
A quick fluff of hair. A dab of scent
to keep his olfactory keen. Poor man
his black bag didn't stand a chance

Not with her black cat watching –
Eyes uncannily as her own
as she whipped the quicksilver
all around the living-room floor.

Because

Because love is stronger than fear
here I am again, riding the turbulences
to see my sister in the USA.
The warring-air.

Six thousand feet above the Atlantic
I sit back trying to keep the charred
memories at bay. Pulling the
little plane window down

Like a shutter on my imagination.
But the red claw of suffering
soon pulls me back into the glare.
And suddenly,

Amidst the remembered blood and flames
the miles and miles of horror
the scream I never uttered
threatens to surface in a pressurised cabin –

Stay calm. Stay calm dear heart.
Picture a safe landing.
The emergence from this cocoon
into a sister's smiling.

John
O'Donoghue

John O'Donoghue's work includes 'The Beach Generation' and 'Brunch Poems'. A memoir, 'Sectioned', will be published by John Murray in 2009.

I first met Brian Behan in 1995, when I organised an Irish Festival that became the hit of that year's Brighton Festival. I got hold of his number and phoned him. 'I'd be delighted to take part,' he declared, asking for neither money nor contract. Brian's play, 'Hallelujah I'm A Bum!' was playing that year in the Pavilion Theatre. A journalist friend of Brian's called Tory Central Office to protest about the play.

Brian was denounced by the desk jockey at Tory HQ, which played right into the journalist's hands. Brian got two great columns in The Independent, full of quotes from his Tory patsy, who went bonkers when he heard about the scene in which 'Mr Portaloo' is caught having the PM over his desk. All of Brian's houses were sold out and the events he took part in for me were rammed.

When Brian died in November 2002, I wanted to remember this great son of Ireland. The Behans – Brendan, Dominic and Brian – were all fine singers and it was in song that I wanted to commemorate him. Song belongs to the people in ways sometimes that poetry does not. There was sadness at his funeral, but also a kind of loving joy. His daughters and first wife Celia all spoke eloquently and affectionately about him. I knew him to be a man you could not help but love. I was lucky to count Brian as my friend.

Brighton is a much quieter, much poorer place without him.

A Song for Brian

O, I went down to Brighton beach
looking out for Brian
ah, but he seemed just out of reach
looking out for Brian

O, Brian, Brian where've you gone?
where've you gone to Brian?
O, Brian, Brian where've you gone?
can't you hear me cryin'?

I thought I saw him in the sea
looking out for Brian
waving, waving up at me
looking out for Brian

O, Brian, Brian where've you gone?
where've you gone to Brian?
O, Brian, Brian where've you gone?
can't you hear me sighin'?

O, I went out to take the air
looking out for Brian
I couldn't find him anywhere
looking out for Brian

O, Brian, Brian where've you gone?
where've you gone to Brian?
O, Brian, Brian where've you gone?
can't you hear me cryin'?

I thought I saw him on his bike
looking out for Brian
ah, have you ever seen his like
looking out for Brian

O, Brian, Brian where've you gone?
where you've gone to Brian?
O, Brian, Brian, where've you gone?
can't you hear me sighin'?

They say that Brian's dead and gone,
there'll be no more of Brian -
come and help me sing my song,
come and help me Brian.

On The Death Of A Surfer

The wave that took him was the wave he craved,
It curled around him as he surfed to his death;
The rain falls down on the drowned and the saved.

We saw him ride the whitecaps, and we raved
About the cool way he moved like a breath:
The wave that took him was the wave he craved.

It came like a sigh and though we all waved,
Called out, he seemed to be blind, to be deaf:
The rain falls down on the drowned and the saved.

Write this in the sand, have it engraved:
He rose like a sun that hasn't yet set.
The wave that took him was the wave he craved.

Surfing's as deep as the sea – he was enslaved,
Not by the waves, but by their deadly roulette.
The rain falls down on the drowned and the saved.

Now his board's his gravestone, and the earth's waived
All right to him. What we saw we'll never forget:
The wave that took him, the wave that he craved;
The rain falling down on the drowned and the saved.

Cricket At Arundel

Sussex vs Hampshire

Here where the kiss of willow
  Knocks on the leather ball
I lie upon a pillow
  Of grass and I watch it all.

I watch the airy summer clouds,
  The players at the crease,
The slow parade of ambling crowds,
  The reasonableness, the peace.

Amidst a grove of English trees
  Around the cricket pitch
The lightest of melodies
  Floats up low and rich.

The sound of summer gentling folk
  Who've come to see the sport,
To laze like me, to laugh and joke –
  Green shades, green hills, green thoughts.

And though a noisy chopper
  Might racket overhead –
Loud, rude and improper –
  For us the globe is red.

It's held in Shane Warne's spinning hands,
  A compressed English sun,
Flying through the air to land
  As Adams gets a run.

Blissful, sunny, country prospect,
  An Eden all our own,
Here where bat and ball connect
  And Sussex are at home.

6th June 2007

Catherine Smith

Catherine was chosen as one of the 'Next Generation' poets of 2004 by the PBS/Arts Council. Her first full collection, 'The Butcher's Hands' (Smith/Doorstop) was a PBS recommendation. A new collection, 'Lip', is forthcoming from Smith/Doorstop in November 2007 and a collection of her short stories will be published by Bluechrome next year.

New direction....I'm concerned with time and how slippery it is. And how memory can be at the same time 'personally' accurate and yet an illusion. There are quite a few references to roads, railways and airports in recent poems. I like motorways - the fact they act like arteries, linking bits of the body/country. Service stations are very strange and hopeful places for me. I once had a major personal epiphany at Clacket Lane on the M25. Every time I go back there I hope for a similarly enlightening experience, but it's never happened since.

Thirst

For Graham Stewart

And now I'm sitting at the wrong end of the train and
the drinks trolley may never get here, I might
alight at Victoria with my tongue like sandpaper,

my belly growling like an engine. I sigh, straining
to hear its rattle, its tantalising chink, chink, chink,
its louche promises of peanuts, gin, tonic, ice and

there's the agony of imagining some fat sod
in carriage G, dithering over cheese and tomato
or ham and mustard on white - bastard! - as if

they weren't already dull enough, doughy enough,
indulged enough. I mop my damp brow, I'm so
unreasonable, I'm becoming a petulant bigot but

if the damned trolley doesn't get here before Gatwick
the time it takes to pour, sip and properly savour
will be lost and after all, it's well known a poet needs

a mainly liquid diet and so when it finally arrives,
when it crunches to my seat I'm weak and silly with relief,
I'm pathetic, parched, a spiteful, snarling camel,

I check with the man there's ice (ready to spit if there isn't),
I have the money ready, I meet his kind eyes and say,
too loud, Oh, thank God! I thought you'd never ask.

The Sanctification Of Clacket Lane Services, Westbound

It's done overnight, without fuss
- a Midnight blessing, holy water sprinkled
onto formica and pine, in dim light.
So, by morning, Costa's cappuccinos
have become the blood of Christ
for slumped Sales Managers
who stare at the car-park wondering
how their waistlines disappeared under
a soft mulch of fat, why their wives
no longer kiss them fully on the lips.
It's now a new Cathedral
for the transient congregations, floods
of hungry, whey-faced souls washed up
into its halls, its echoing corridors –
teenagers texted by the Holy Spirit,
games machines suddenly luminous
with the Annunciation, Gabriel's hand
on Mary's shoulder. The dark recesses
of the Gents are places of confession,
men mouthing silently, their brows
unclenched. The blessing of a particular tap,
in the Ladies' means hot water flowing
over a woman's hands leaves her
with a sense of purity, peace,
her palms free of the taint of money
she'd used to pacify the kids –
for burgers, fries, and mega-cokes
black as Priests' robes. And when
those customers leave, redeemed,
the drone and burr of traffic will soothe
like Plainsong, or a call to prayer.

The Lost Cats

Standing by the baggage carousel, I'm becoming increasingly anxious
about my bag, which is not among
all the other bags in our party's luggage. I'm with the band,
it's been a long, gruelling tour, and
most of them are in the Gents snorting coke with the Tech guys -
apart from the dead ones, who are still
knocking back Dom Perignon in the Club Class bar.
The carousel slumps around, piled with
the lead singer's five Burberry checked matching cases, I drag them off,
where the hell is my bag, I need to know -
I'd recognise its battered green leather anywhere, the family crest,
two crossed machetes - and there's still no sign -
which is terrible because this morning I packed the cats in it -
I nested them among my soiled knickers
and sweat-grimed tee-shirts, they haven't been fed
since Reyjavik. They're barely more than kittens,
tortoiseshell, with milky blue eyes, semi-feral, I won them in a poker game
and feel responsible. Maybe the bag wasn't loaded,
maybe it's heading for Dalaman, perhaps some kindly baggage handler
liberated them and is in the process
of reporting the incident,
or maybe they've escaped and, somewhere in the bowels
of the airport, they're already, incestuously,
fucking urgently, the boy cat biting the girl cat's neck,
among dust-balls and heating ducts.
Before we know it
Gatwick will be over-run with cats, curled asleep in waiting areas, rubbing
against the legs of cabin crew, running amok
on runways.
This is freaking me out. I flail my arms, attract the attention
of a man in uniform, nonchalant and tall, with
little wings on his jacket.
My bag's gone missing, I tell him, and the thing is -
He shakes his head and produces a pale blue form.
Oh, don't tell me, he says wearily, handing me a gold-tipped fountain pen,
cats, right? Yes, I admit, ashamed, cats.

The Biting Point

Thirty years dead and still curmudgeonly,
my grandfather is driving me through
the fog-numbed streets of Crystal Palace
at five a.m. He's in the plaid dressing gown
he wore to die in, and he's shaved,
badly, flecks of dark blood stippling his chin.
We're the only Austin 1100 on the road;
he tuts, crunching through the gears,
he blames the damp, the bad oil,
the years it sat cobwebbed in a garage.
My grandfather slows for the lights,
not best pleased when the engine stalls –
it's no part of his plan, I know,
to crank the key three times before
the damned thing fires – the times he's told me
a good driver knows his car's temperament
like the back of his hand. As a milk float
toots behind us, he mutters, frowns,
eases one foot off the clutch as
the other trembles over the accelerator.
Listen to that! He's triumphant
as the engine warbles its surprise –
Better than any opera! he says, and then
That's known as the biting point,
I'm just telling you so's when you get
a husband, you'll know what's what.
We coast down Fountain Drive, the car
sighs and dreams, a purring baby now.
My grandfather's bolt upright, sliding
the wheel under calloused palms
as the BBC transmitter winks in the distance -
the last thing he mentioned, the last fixed light.

Lorna Thorpe

Lorna Thorpe's debut poetry collection from Pighog Press 'Dancing To Motown' was the Poetry Book Society's pamphlet choice for autumn 2005. Also a published short story and features writer, her first full collection, 'A Ghost In My House', is due from Arc this year.

How I came to write 'The Crime of the Century'? I was online, researching 'lightning' for a poem I was writing and ended up reading about electric chairs. I knew about the Rosenbergs, of course, but I didn't know it took five shocks to kill Ethel. I write a lot of poems about love and its disappointments but rarely about other people. But I was hooked by a photograph of the couple kissing after their arraignment and a report about a meeting they had with their lawyer on death row, when they virtually tore one another's clothes off. That meeting became my starting point. At one stage I reversed the order of the last two stanzas – finishing with the electrocution created too neat an ending.

There are a lot of mouths in this poem. Ethel's tight, darkly painted lips had fascinated me from the start but I'd never intended to make them a motif. Several drafts down the line it dawned on me that mouths had a greater significance. Anti-Communist hysteria was certainly to blame for their appalling execution, but the couple's stoic silence in court also played its part.

Still, I suspect that's not the whole story behind the mouths. As I write this, I'm probing an ulcer on my cheek with my tongue. My mouth is one of my weak spots. I didn't set out to write about love and silence, a recurring theme of my own work and life, but these things have a way of insinuating themselves into your lines. For me, that's where the magic lies – in all the hidden stuff going on behind the scenes.

The Most Beautiful Man On Spetse

fed me cherries, talked Plato and Plath, admired
my Bilko tee shirt, that I was reading Don DeLillo.

He had everything I wanted in a Greek god
but I only knew how to be grateful for what I was given.

The night he made me a fruit cocktail
with fresh pineapple and melon, I was tarted up

for a disco in Milton Keynes. Flashing plastic
smiles and heels, I demanded ouzo and lots of it.

Ah, the hit of that cloudy gut rot, the satisfaction
of screwing a boy with a first in football trivia, who bragged

to the entire island. My Greek god never fed me
cherries again but what the hell, it was time to move on.

Trying To Love The View From Bella Veduta

What's not to love? Chorus line of olive trees
shimmying at the foot of the hill; ploughed field
fanning out like a bride's veil behind
the skeletal house on the brow; a peach tree
with one wizened fruit, as forlorn and gaudy
as a Christmas bauble in March.
A black and white lizard, so chic
it might have crawled from Wallis Simpson's lapel,
circuits the terrace while the church bells
of Montelparo chime from medieval stone.
Even the Yellow Ballerinas – here every day
at 9.15 sharp – have upped the acrobatics this morning,
swooping and darting in and out of a fig tree.
It's all so very lovely. And I have loved
some views in my time: the Manhattan skyline
from the far side of Brooklyn Bridge;
ghost towns clinging to the Catalan Pyrenees.
When did I stop loving things?
I'm dying for a little transcendental soaring,
some amber warmth oiling the heart. But here I am
in 90 degrees of shade, mesmerised by the wasp
that bothered my breakfast. It's drowning
in a jug of orange juice, front legs scrabbling
a furious doggy paddle, face pressed
against the glass, as if pleading for its life.

Bluebeard's Momentos

The porn comes as a relief, a smudge
on the flawless score card of my husband,
picture book son of parents who play bridge
and golf, whose executive home gleams
with the lustre of the righteous. I'm trying
to live up to them, but always fall short –
smashed glass, scraped fenders, sticky rings
in store cupboards, ghost stains
of that other lifetime, that other me.
So these Technicolor loves,
refugees of the spare room's forbidden city
bring some spread-eagled hope.
He's not perfect.
But then, the paper coffins. Photos
of a blonde Venus, a poem about Elysian Fields,
valentine message in the card he drove 500 miles
to deliver, mention of a ring. I had no idea.
Our pasts exiled, another relief –
he would never have married that other girl,
the one with the speed, the acid, the biker
sent down for GBH. I am Eve, already fallen,
falling again, swallowing another secret:
the image bricked up in the blue chamber of his mind,
first-chosen bride, the frozen words
on her ashen lips forever turning him down.

The Crime Of The Century

Burning up inside, Ethel Rosenberg gets dressed
as if she's going to a gala. For one bright moment
everything forgotten: her brother's lies, evidence –
typewriter, console table, notes burning in a frying pan –
as flimsy as her nylons. She remembers only Julie's touch,
his pencilled love letters, the arias she sung him
from an adjoining cell. And then he's there, her husband,
and the room has no screen and they charge and grasp,
mouths, hands, flesh. Prised apart by guards. Julie's face
so smeared with lipstick he looks as if he's bleeding.

That last hot evening, their fourteenth anniversary,
they finger kiss through wire mesh, blood trickling
down the screen. At 8.06, just before the setting sun
heralds the Jewish Sabbath over Sing-Sing, Julius is dead.
Minutes later, Ethel, in a green print dress, settles
tight lips into a Mona Lisa smile. Says nothing,
winces as the electrode cap makes contact with her skull.
It takes five shocks to kill her, the oak chair made
for a man, Ethel so petite the helmet doesn't fit, so fried
witnesses see coils of smoke rising from her head.

She dreamed of being an opera singer but who was she
to have such dreams, product of the Jewish Bronx,
a mother who belittled her, said she brought it on herself?
Anyway, her mouth would never open wide enough,
except to kiss him, her beloved Julius. His crime?
Handing over minor secrets. Hers was finding love
one New Year's Eve, just before she went onstage to sing.
He cooled her flaming nerves. Never having known such caring
she hurled herself into her role – loyal wife, so insignificant
to the KGB, she didn't even have a code name.

Sarah
Wardle

Sarah is lecturer in poetry at Middlesex University and has published two collections with Bloodaxe, 'Fields Away', shortlisted for the Forward prize for best first collection, and 'SCORE!', which includes some of her poems, written as poet-in-residence for Tottenham Hotspur Football Club. She has just finished her third collection.

'Responsibility' and 'Guy Fawkes from Ebury Ward' are part of a series of poems, written during a long spell in a psychiatric hospital. There was not much to do and writing helped to keep me sane and enabled me to keep my job, although I had great help from my family, boyfriend, the Responsible Medical Officer, ward doctor, nurses and the University and College Union representatives, and even from my workplace, Middlesex University.

I have friends of all religions and my forename is originally Hebrew. I did not choose to be baptised, as I was too young to have a say, but I did choose not to be confirmed and I do not wish to be married, but I should very much like a large family and this is problematic, because I am going to be thirty-eight years old next week and, if one counts from conception, I already am! I also have to withdraw from Diazepam and Risperidone.

I miss my dead grandmother, but I am very lucky to have my parents, living grandmother, aunt, uncle and great-aunt and my boyfriend and very good friends.

I recently was put in charge of someone with a drink problem for the night, as the N.H.S. did not have a bed for him and that was funny because a manic was looking after an alcoholic! We laughed. There is not enough laughter in the world of poetry. However, poetry reminds one of the dark occasions of life, and death, and it is best not to forget these.

Guy Fawkes From Ebury Ward

So many times I've watched the Bonfire Boyes
process with torch-lit pitch down Battle High Street,
and enjoyed the crowd's rebellion of spirit,
yet this evening, shut up on a mental ward,

the sound of ideological bomb fire
seems to complain of Iraq and America,
whilst anti-Catholic arguments grow tired
in the candle glow of Westminster Cathedral's spire.

Granddaddy

after Sylvia Plath

I imagine my grandfathers talking to me
down the decades after they died,
one who left before I was conceived,
one who went when I was five,
into the future they'll never see
wishing me well, that I'll survive
the highs and lows. Would I have believed
in Father and Son, had they been alive?
The fact is their widows struggled on
to one hundred, and ninety-two and counting.
Fairy Grandmother Nature is my religion,
who simply leaves white wizards standing.
But somewhere Gandalf is standing near
and my own father, I hope, shall be a grandfather.

Responsibility

after Rabbi Jonathan Sacks

This mental hospital is an almshouse
for the homeless, drunk, divorced, down-and-out.
Before I came here I knew little of
strangers who have a sense of moral love

and although I have rejected Christianity,
I feel an older Biblical responsibility
to help the ill and suffering through life
as part of the Whole, which we each comprise,

so that ethics can turn the firmament upright,
rethink priorities and review sight,
turning cynicism, hedonism and stoicism
into positive humanitarianism and altruism,

letting humans see acts not as their own,
but as stemming from and leading to the One,
healing flaws in the universe,
so that we can repair what once was worse,

upholding a respect for tradition,
handing wisdom down each generation,
transforming the afflicted, lonely and sick
into creatures we were created to be with.

North West London

July, 2004

As I walked uphill through Gladstone Park
on the hottest day of the year, I thought of you
in the heatwave of '69, before the first steps
of a man on the moon, and a giant leap for me
and you, since this July you were in the States,
where back in '68 you conceived me,

when still too young to imagine fully
what it would mean when they gave me to you,
and despite forgetting my A to Z, a sixth sense
took me in the right direction, as a carriage
drawn by two black horses with white plumes
sped by with a white bride and black groom,

and when on the verge of giving up and waiting
at the nearest bus stop, I asked a young family
going by where the site of the nursing home was,
their father pointed to feet from where I stood,
a housing estate called Pippin Close,
indicating the gateposts, 1911, each with a slot

and the inscription, Donations for the Hospital,
though we know a Sister there was not giving,
how that nun withdrew her hand as you were
holding on and out through labour pains,
when I was taken from you by forceps, the cord
round my neck, so that even now I was feeling

its umbilical tug, though you were again that day
air miles across the Atlantic, and as I saw layers
of paint like skin, peeling through black to grey,
and red to rust, like hair to ashes, flesh to dust,
and stepped into absent gates, like a womb,
before exiting again in a secular rebirth,

like a comet's return past the earth, after an orbit
of half my three score years and ten, just then
the carriage and black horses with white plumes,
bearing the white bride and black groom, trotted
by once more, their marriage dusted and done,
and I boarded a red bus back into town.

Jackie
Wills

Jackie's fourth collection of poetry 'Commandments', is published by Arc this autumn. It covers territory that she has always been interested in – people and relationships – but in this one she expands into religion and how a woman defines herself. Her first collection, 'Powder Tower', was shortlisted for the 1995 TS Eliot prize. Other collections are 'Party' (Leviathon 2000) and 'Fever Tree' (Arc 2003).

Of 'Breton Wedding Dress' she writes "I first tried to write it about 20 years ago. It's based in truth, in so far as I did once wear someone else's black velvet dress but of course, for any woman, it's such a loaded image. I think I've made about five versions of this poem at different stages of my life and abandoned them all. Earlier this year, though, I began a piece of fiction based on the summer when I wore this dress. The Fest Noz of the first line has become a key part of this narrative - a time when the story turns. I wonder if I needed to complete this poem in order to somehow free the story? There's no doubt in my mind that the writing of this poem and the fiction are linked, but I'm not entiely sure how or why. Eventually, the route in was the physicality of the dress and accessories and the smell of farm cider, keeping the poem momentary and brief".

To My Daughter

I dedicate a cathedral of candles –
each blackened chapel,
altar, rose window, saint, reliquary,

breath of frankincense, every flame
between fingertips,
every shadow drawn by fire.

Balance

Did an alarm
beep unnoticed

when the years I had left
were equal to those I'd lived,

when past and future
were as balanced

as a chunk of butter
and a four ounce weight?

The Grass Is Long On My Allotment

Nothing for autumn but onions,
potatoes, chard. There may be leeks
if weeds don't choke the seedlings.
St David won't help, nor whatever god
stretches brambles over raspberries,
twists bindweed around stems
and the wind doesn't cry Mary -
there's no subject but him, no address
but his, no other name to swallow.

Breton Wedding Dress

Before the Fest Noz, the farmer's widow
unfolds her wedding dress from a chest,
holds it up – heavy black velvet.
I step into the skirt, she buttons the back.
Next, a green apron edged in ivy,
white lace cap, two silver barrettes.
She pours a tumbler of cider, cloudy, tart,
toasts the three of us: the girl she was,
and me, arms linked in her eldest son's,
shows me the steps I'll need to dance.

THE SOUTH. Creative writing

THE SOUTH is a friendly organisation that has fun with words. We're a not for profit writers' network and literary arts agency that develops projects, talent, audiences, readers and communities in Brighton & Hove, Sussex and the south of England.

Through our regular events and workshops, and the Brighton International Poetry Festival, we have played a special role in promoting poetry and poets based in the south of England.

We always welcome the opportunity of working in partnership whether locally, regionally, nationally or internationally. Our partnership projects include Brighton Children's Book Festival, Runnymede International Literary Festival Community and Education Programme and the Pulse Europoem project.

We offer a network of services including:
Creative writing workshops of all types
Community, education and literacy projects
Landscape and heritage writing projects
Event and festival organisation
Project management & consultancy
Networking and advice
Professional development
Meeting space at Brighton Writers' Centre.

For more information about our activities please see **www.thesouth.org.uk**

THE SOUTH
Brighton Writers' Centre
49 Grand Parade
Brighton BN2 9QA
UK
01273 571700

Afterword

POETRY SOUTH?
What's that then?

Literature organisation THE SOUTH was set up in 2002 when the government ordained regions of the South East and the South West seemed set to obliterate any tentative idea of the South as a cultural or geo-political entity. But THE SOUTH was also a tongue in cheek reaction to the idea of the North and to the conflation that the south equates to and includes London.

Is there a definably southern poetry, a southern voice? Is there a definable southern literature? Could it, does it express a regional identity and multi-culture? Can it bring to life a sense of place? Is it essentially reactionary to the North as the stronger cultural brand? Does it matter anyway or is it mere parochialism in an era of globalisation?

These are the kind of questions THE SOUTH asks and that lie behind this fascinating anthology of contemporary poetry in English, written by poets based in the south of England.

In the melee of crossed boundaries, changed identity, lost directions and new opportunity THE SOUTH typifies the state of flux in which we all find ourselves,struggling to voice the voiceless and be heard.